Healthy Eating

Wayne Jackman

Healthy Living

Healthy Teeth
Healthy Hair
Healthy Skin
Healthy Eyes
Healthy Hands and Feet
Healthy Eating

Words printed in **bold** are explained in the glossary

First published in 1990 by
Wayland (Publishers) Limited
61 Western Road, Hove
East Sussex, BN3 1JD, England

Consultant: Diana Bentley, Reading
Consultant, University of Reading
Editor: James Kerr

British Library Cataloguing in Publication Data
Jackman, Wayne
  Healthy eating
  1. Man. Health. Effects of diet
  I. Title II. Series
  613.2

  ISBN 1–85210–929–7

Typeset by N. Taylor, Wayland Publishers Limited
Printed and bound by Casterman S.A., Belgium

Contents

Why we should eat healthily

Most babies are first fed on baby milk. It contains exactly the right balance of nutrients that a baby needs.

Nutrients are the substances in food and drink which give you energy and help you grow healthily. They also protect you from illness.

As you grow older, you need to eat food that will give you the right balance of nutrients. This will keep you healthy just as milk did when you were a baby.

4

A balanced **diet** helps you to grow strong, fight **infection**, and to work and play. Food is like the petrol in

a car: it makes you go. Without enough healthy food, you would be tired, weak and miserable. Then you might easily get ill. As well as keeping the outside of your body clean and healthy, you must look after the inside. Eating healthily keeps the inside and outside of your body well.

What is healthy eating?

Have you ever heard the saying 'you are what you eat'?
It means that if you eat healthily you will be healthy.

These are the nutrients that a healthy diet should have, and some foods which contain one or more of them:

- FAT – found in butter, cheese and vegetable oil.
- STARCH – found in cereals, bread and rice.
- PROTEIN – found in fish, meat, milk and nuts.
- VITAMINS – C (found in oranges), A (found in carrots).
- MINERALS – iron (found in liver and spinach), calcium (found in milk).
- FIBRE – found in fruit, vegetables and cereals.
- WATER.

A sensible balance of these nutrients will keep you fit and healthy. You should not eat too much of any one thing, like sugary biscuits or chips. You can still eat all of your favourite foods, like hamburgers, but try to cut down on them. Try to eat more fresh fruit, vegetables and cereals instead.

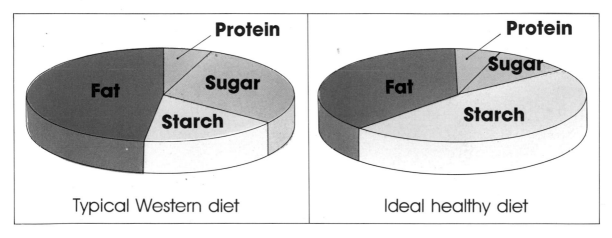

Typical Western diet | Ideal healthy diet

How diet affects your body

Your diet affects your whole body. If you eat healthily then all the **organs** inside your body will work properly. Your heart will be strong and your **bowels** will easily get rid of waste.

Diet affects the outside of your body too. Calcium, found in milk and brown bread, will keep your teeth and nails healthy. Vitamin A from eggs and green vegetables will keep your skin smooth and clear.

If you do not eat healthily, it soon shows in your appearance. You may develop a skin **rash** or split nails, and look pale. Foods like vegetables, cereals and milk can prevent infections and illnesses. Without a balanced diet you will feel run-down and easily catch colds.

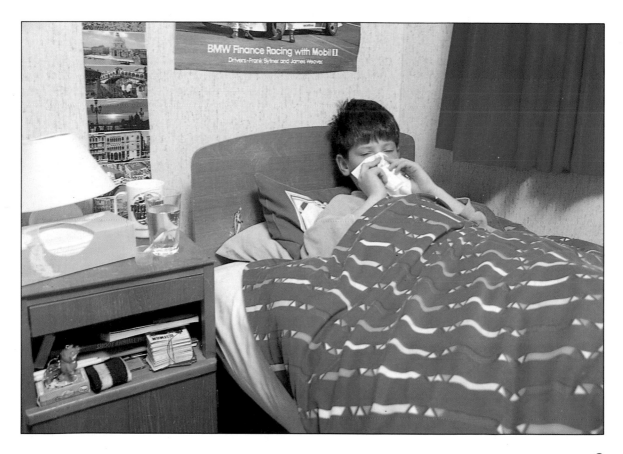

Good eating habits

Here are some dishes that are full of goodness and very tasty too:

- Fresh fruit salad with natural yoghurt.
- Whole-wheat spaghetti bolognese.
- Chicken salad.
- Baked beans on **whole-wheat bread** toast.
- A milk shake made with skimmed milk.

- A bowl of muesli.
- A baked potato with cottage cheese.

What others can you think of?

10

How food is cooked is important. Vegetables should not be boiled because this removes a lot of the goodness. They should be steamed or eaten raw. Meat should be grilled on a wire rack so that most of the fatty oils drain away. Too much fat is bad for you.

Try not to eat snacks like crisps between meals.

Instead of sweets, chew celery or dried fruit. At meal times, eating slowly will stop you getting **indigestion**.

Bad eating habits

Some foods contain a lot of sugar and fat, so you should not eat too much of them.

Here are some foods you should try to cut down on:

- Fried food, like chips and crisps.
- Sugary food, like sweets, biscuits, jam and chocolate.
- Sugar, on cereal or in tea.
- Fizzy pop, like cola and blackcurrant.
- Burgers and sausage-rolls.

- Butter and salad cream.
- White bread and white rice.

12

- Convenience food, like instant soup.
- Salty food, like salted peanuts.

   Biscuits are an 'empty' food because they have such a high amount of sugar. Sugar provides instant energy but this soon wears off. Food with a lot of sugar can make you overweight as well. It is better to snack on fresh fruit like a peach or banana.

   Eating too much is bad for you, and so is skipping meals or eating snacks instead. Try to eat regularly throughout the day.

Keeping food healthy

It is not only important to eat healthy food but you must also store it in a healthy way. Fresh fruit and vegetables are best eaten soon after buying them. If they are stored for too long, they will lose their Vitamin C. Dry food, like rice and pasta, should be stored in airtight containers to keep it fresh. **Perishable** food, like cheese, meat and fish, should be kept in a cold fridge.

Raw meat and fish contain germs that can easily

infect other food. It is important to store meat and fish on separate plates so that no juices drip down on to other food in the fridge.

Food should not be left out uncovered, especially in summer. Flies and other insects love to settle on it, spreading germs. Half-finished cans of food, like baked beans, should be tipped into a small bowl, covered and kept in the fridge.

Many tins and packets are marked with a **sell by date**. If food is past its sell by date, it should be thrown away.

Preparing food healthily

Food should be prepared in a healthy way. Before touching food:

- Hands should be washed and dirty nails scrubbed with a nailbrush.
- Long hair should be tied back.
- Pots and pans used to prepare the food should be checked to make sure they are clean.

Following these simple rules will prevent the spread of germs on to food. Germs can cause upset tummies, **diarrhoea** and **food poisoning**.

Very often, chemicals are sprayed on to fruit and vegetables while they are growing. Wash these off by rinsing the fruit and vegetables under running water. Then you can eat them.

Meat and eggs need to be well cooked to kill off any germs in them, such as **salmonella**. If a microwave oven is being used to cook packaged food, the **cooking instructions** should be followed properly. Under-cooked food can make you ill.

Eating healthily throughout the day

A regular eating pattern throughout the day will keep you healthy. This means having breakfast, lunch and tea or supper. It is very important to eat a good, healthy breakfast such as cereal or an egg with whole-wheat

bread toast. This will 'set you up' for the day, helping you to concentrate and play, especially at school.

If you miss a meal your body will start to run out of energy and you will feel tired. Raw celery, carrots, nuts and dried fruit are all right to nibble between meals as a quick boost, but do not eat too many snacks.

Eating last thing at night is not a good idea. When you fall asleep the food lies in your stomach and is not

burnt up. If the food is not burnt up through exercise, your weight increases.

Eating healthily throughout the year

In the winter your body needs more energy to keep warm. This means that in the winter, people feel like eating large, hot meals such as stews or baked potatoes.

In the summer, when it is warmer, people often eat lighter meals such as salads. Although you need less energy to keep warm in the summer, you might play sports and go swimming more often. This means that you still need to eat a balanced, healthy diet to give you energy.

20

When it is hot you should drink more. Your body needs about two litres of water every day. Some of this comes from food such as tomatoes and cucumbers, but you still need to drink plenty of liquids.

Try different foods as they come into season: turnips and swedes in winter, raspberries and watermelons in summer.

Being a vegetarian

Vegetarians are people who do not eat meat, although some eat fish. A vegetarian diet can be just as tasty as a diet which includes meat.

Although meat contains nutrients your body needs, a mixture of food from plants, such as whole-wheat bread and lentil soup, will keep you just as healthy. In fact, soya beans contain the same nutrients as meat and are often used in vegetarian recipes. Some hamburger restaurants even sell beanburgers!

If you are a vegetarian, it is important that you eat a wide variety of dairy products, beans, nuts, fruit,

vegetables and cereals. These will give you all the nutrients that you need. One young person out of every six is a vegetarian.

Different shapes

Everyone has a different body shape. Some people are broader or heavier than others. It does not mean that they are unhealthy, it is just the shape and weight they are. Many young people have **puppy fat**. This is a natural part of growing up and they will lose this fat when they are older.

Some people have a fast **metabolism**. This means that their bodies burn up food very quickly, to produce energy. They can eat a lot and remain the same shape.

Other people have a slower metabolism. They have to be careful because if they eat too much, they will become overweight. A **dietician** can help people to get back to a healthy weight by changing their diet.

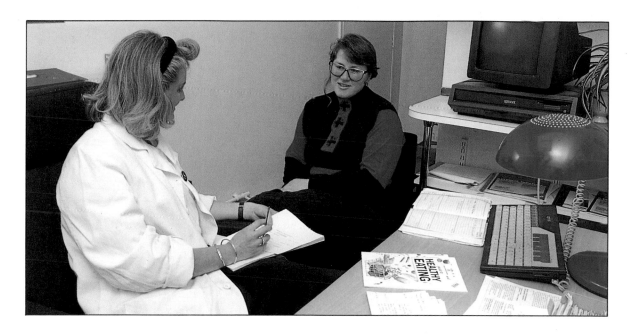

Some people are thin because they do not eat enough. This is unhealthy because they will not have enough energy to work and play. A doctor can help people with this problem to return to a healthy weight.

Whatever shape you are, exercise is very important. Exercise burns up the food you eat and stops you putting on weight. It also keeps your blood-pressure down, which keeps you healthy.

Food allergies and illnesses

Some people have **allergic reactions** when they eat certain foods. If you suffer from **eczema**, then this may be an allergic reaction to something you have eaten. Shellfish sometimes brings people out in a rash, and chocolate can cause bad headaches called **migraines**.

If you suffer from eczema or rashes, there are special tests that a doctor can do to see if they are caused by

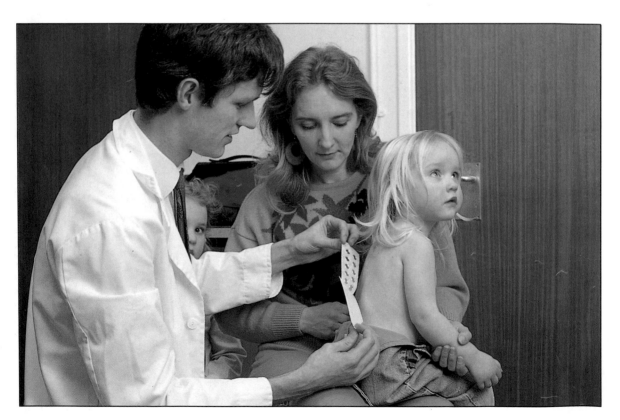

food. You may need to stop eating a particular type of food. People with **diabetes** have to be careful about the amount of sugar they eat.

Certain foods, such as some cakes and biscuits contain additives . These are chemicals which preserve and colour food, but they can be bad for you. Lists of ingredients on packets and tins of food show how many additives the foods contain. Foods with too many should be avoided.

Eating for a healthy life

It is important to form good eating habits when you are young. Look back through this book and remember which foods are good for you. You might need to change your diet. If you do, start today.

Try especially to cut down on the amount of fatty and sugary foods that you eat. In the Western world the

biggest cause of death is heart-disease. This is caused by eating too much fat!

Healthy eating should keep your body healthy right up to old age. Look after it – it is the only one you have got!

Glossary

Allergic reactions Blotches on skin, sneezing, or other reactions caused by something you are sensitive to.

Bowels The part of your body that gets rid of solid waste.

Cooking instructions A series of directions telling you how to cook food properly.

Diabetes An illness caused by too much sugar in the blood.

Diarrhoea An illness which upsets your stomach and makes you go to the toilet often.

Diet The food and drink that you regularly eat and drink.

Dietician A person who specializes in diet. Dieticians advise people how to eat healthily.

Eczema A disease of the skin.

Food poisoning An illness caused by eating food that is naturally poisonous or has gone bad.

Indigestion An upset stomach, caused by eating too quickly.

Infection An illness.

Metabolism The process in your body which produces energy.

Migraines Very bad headaches.

Organs The inside parts of your body, like your heart and liver.

Perishable Something which will rot over a period of time. Meat is perishable, plastic is not.

Puppy fat Plumpness in some young children.

Rash Blotches on the skin.

Salmonella Germs which cause food poisoning.

Sell by date The day when food starts to go stale or rotten.

Whole-wheat bread Bread made from the whole grains of wheat. It is much better for you than white bread.

Books to read

Diet and Nutrition by Brian R. Ward (Franklin Watts, 1987)

Health and Food by Dorothy Baldwin (Wayland, 1987)

The Human Body by Jonathan Miller and David Pelham (Jonathan Cape, 1983)

You and Your Food by Judy Tatchell & Dilys Wells (Usborne, 1985)

Your Body Fuel by Dorothy Baldwin & Claire Lister (Wayland, 1983)

Index

Picture acknowledgements

All photographs by Trevor Hill except cover ZEFA, 27 Paul Seheult. Artwork by John Yates.